The 7 Principles of Success:

How To Use Them To Live The Life Of Your Dreams

By Joshua S. Kangley

To Presley and Nora, may the light always shine on your Purpose.

"Life is really simple, but we insist on making it complicated."

--Confucius

The 7 Principles of Success:

How To Use Them To Live The Life Of Your Dreams
By Joshua S. Kangley

Table of Contents

Prologue

Before I begin with these 7 powerful Principles, I want to thank you, personally, for taking the time to read my book. I should tell you straight away that I'm no doctor. I'm also not a psychologist or nutritionist. In fact, I never finished college so I don't even have a degree, in anything, at all. Period. At this point, you may be questioning why you should even read this book then. **Here is why you should definitely read this book in its entirety: I shouldn't be writing it.** All the odds were against me and I could have easily up ended up being a statistic. If I hadn't applied these 7 Principles in my life, in fact, I believe I would have been dead by now. I don't want to get into all the details here (that's perhaps another book). But, to make a very long story very short, I experienced a lot of trauma as a child, and growing up I don't think I could fully process some of it. Eventually, I turned to drugs and alcohol as a sort of escape. This escape turned into abuse and I got so bad that my pastor once told me, "You're going to end up in jail or dead if you keep going on like this."

Obviously, I'm not dead or I wouldn't be writing this, and God willing, I will live a long time yet to see my beautiful daughters grow up. But I did land in jail. It wasn't long after I had that talk with my pastor that I was behind bars. Though I'm not at all proud of that jailtime, I'm thankful for it. It was there that I turned my life around. I haven't shared that with many people and there will be many who will be surprised that I was in jail. I have hidden this fact about myself for a long time. I spent years working on myself and getting as far away as I could from my past. However, I have realized that it's in owning this experience and sharing it that I can truly make a difference and help others.

So, the very fact that a guy who should be dead went to jail, turned his life around and became successful, should be the very reason you should read this book. I truly believe that if you read and comprehend these Principles, you'll find some guidance in them. If you then apply that guidance to your life, you'll live happier, healthier, and more successfully. My Purpose for this book is to reach those who have been at the bottom or have had tough times and are looking for some tools and resources to turn things around. I'm here to prove to you that it IS possible. If I can do it, I know you can, too. This book entails the 7 Principles that I believe anyone can use, no matter where you are or have been. I thank you for picking up this book and I encourage you to read on with an open heart and mind. That all said, I would like to say again that I'm not in any way professionally licensed to give any advice about any serious life events. My eBook should in no way serve as advice or treatment. If you're suffering serious medical issues in any way, I urge you to seek out professional help immediately. If you're ready to take a look at the 7 Principles that I have learned and are willing to apply them in your life, please read on.

Principle 1: Purpose

"The two most important days in life
are the day you're born and the day
you discover the reason why"
--Mark Twain

There's something profound that happens when you start living your life with Purpose. To describe it is difficult, unless you have personally experienced this change. For me, it feels like the Universe literally shifts, and life makes more sense. It's like all the dots in your life are connected and a deeper meaning is understood. To put it another way, when you live your life with a sense of Purpose and live it on purpose, you're living in a higher state of awareness. The meaning of your life and how you connect to it and others makes sense to you. It's in this "higher state of awareness" where you'll live a more successful and happier life. I know those of you reading this who have discovered your purpose can relate to having this "aha" moment. When you're living in your Purpose on purpose, you're living a life full of "aha" moments. I know this may initially seem like a lot of abstract nonsense talk, but MY Purpose for writing this book is to show you that this is real and that you can change your life and start living it to the fullest. It all starts here—discovering your true Purpose.

I started with the Principle of Purpose first because it's the most important of all. That's not to say that the others are not important, **because you need to have all 7 Principles of Success firing in unison for you to reach success and maximize potential.** But, if you don't have Purpose, it will be very difficult to stay motivated on your journey to success. It's indeed a journey and you have made the very first step on this path which I congratulate you for and I'm excited for you. There will be some obstacles on your journey and I want to be honest right away with you about this, but I encourage you to read this book from beginning to end and keep an open mind. Read all 7 Principles discussed in this book and reread them at least once more. The second time around you'll pick up a nugget or two of wisdom or something that speaks to your heart that you missed the first time around.

As I mentioned in the Prologue, I ended up in jail at the age of 18—just out of high school. Again, I don't want to get too deep in the situational details, because that's a whole new book and I want to stick to our subject here. But, to make a very long story short, the turmoil from my childhood had caught up with me in my high school years. I was hanging out with a bad crowd, getting into all sorts of trouble. Essentially, I was living without Purpose. I was letting all those traumatic childhood experiences control my behavior. This is important—**I was living in a reactive state of mind**, instead of living in a proactive state of mind, which happens naturally when you're living in your Purpose on purpose, I was in a state of reaction. You see, I had been pent up with all this anger, confusion, and hurt. I never dealt with the trauma. I didn't have anyone to talk to and I was afraid that either no one would believe me or they would look at me differently—so I just packed it down as far as I could. Let me tell you, that does not work. It never will, because sooner or later it's going to come up and manifest itself in your life in a negative way. For me, it was drugs and alcohol. I started out using them to keep the pain down and forget. That led to abuse and from there spiraled my life completely out of control. I encourage you to deal with issues in your life. Dig deep and get all that out of you. Find someone, anyone that you can talk to, or seek help from a professional. There's no shame in this. I used to believe that it was a weakness, but now I know that seeking help and bettering yourself is strength and it gives you more control in your life. The more control you have of your emotions and decisions equals living more and more in a proactive state of mind rather than reactive, which puts you on the track to finding your Purpose.

So, I was living in this constant state of reaction and defense. What was happening was that this state of mind was clouding reality. So, you can see now that it's hard to find Purpose when you're not really living with a clear mind and a clear reality. Because I never dealt with my emotions and with what happened as a child, my reactionary mindset led me to hurt others and people who really cared about me, and worst yet, hurt myself. I was on a purposeless path of self-destruction and that path led me straight to jail. It was inevitable just like my pastor had warned me.

Now, I understand that some, if not most, of the readers are not in the same situation I was in and perhaps cannot relate to that. I admit, my experience was extreme and I say this, not to dismiss your experience, because I believe we all experience pain, and hurt, and suffering in different ways—but pain is pain, suffering is suffering, and hurt is hurt. I say this however, to point out that just because my experience was extreme trauma, your experience is just as important and no matter where you are in life or where you come from, you can benefit from these Principles of Success. Let me prove to you, by reading this book, that if I can achieve success and happiness, then anyone can. I believe in you and your abilities. So, if you don't have a story that's like mine, you already have a leg up and this book is important to you because if I can turn my life around and achieve massive success, then just imagine what you can do! To those readers who have similar childhood experiences and found themselves making terrible decisions later in life, this book is important to you because if I can turn my life around and achieve massive success, then I have proven that you can too! Even if you have been to the bottom, no matter where you've been or where you are in life now, you can bring yourself back up. These Principles may seem simple and my approach may be different. But, if you read them, understand them, and apply them to your life, the results you'll see will be profound.

Okay, so back to Purpose. How do you find it? How do you know you're living in Purpose? Well, to find your purpose, you must first be open to it. You must also be in a clear state of mind. That's why I suggested that if you're currently in a state of reaction you must clear yourself. This might actually take some time. It took me years to finally come to grips with what was holding me down. The minute I got to jail was the minute I changed my life. I knew instantly I never wanted to come back and that I was going to do all I could to change my life and get it together. Now, just because I had made that decision didn't mean I knew what my Purpose was— that would come almost two decades later. Like I said, I turned my life around once I got out, but it was the decisions I made when I was inside that made me change my life. I went back to school and finished my high school diploma. I went on to do some college and for the next almost 20 years tried to bury that period of time behind me. At this point you may be saying, well, you changed your life around without even discovering your Purpose, so what's the point? Here is where having all the 7 Principles of Success come in to play. **Even if you apply just one of the 7 Principles, you'll experience a Positive change. That's how powerful they are**. And, yes, it's true that the motivation to never be in jail again became a Passion, and that Passion to prove myself was powerful enough to carry me for a while. But, without the other six Principles, it didn't get me to a true level of success. Because without the other six, whenever I was faced with obstacles or challenges, I experienced setbacks. To put it another way, like I said, even just applying any one of the 7 Principles will deliver a positive and powerful change in your life, **but that momentum will fade unless you're applying all 7 of these powerful Principles.** You'll get stuck in a perpetual cycle of ups and downs. You need to fire on all cylinders, so to speak, to reach the finish line. So, I was using motivation, which is part of the Principle of Passion (I will discuss more on this Principle in another chapter) to get me out of the negative situation I was in and turn my life around. That worked for a while and it helped me figure out what my Purpose was. Over a decade later, I finally realized what my purpose was. After running from the fact that I was in jail for fear that people would think less of me, I discovered that the very thing I was running from was my Purpose. Not jail, I'm not running back to jail anytime soon! My experience. I discovered that my purpose is to help others overcome their past and give them tools for success. I put together these Principles of Success that I used to get me from a very dark place in life to help me achieve success. If I can help just one other person, that's my Purpose. So, this book is written with the purpose of helping those at the bottom looking for help. But, I believe that anyone who uses these Principles and applies them will achieve greater success.

You may notice that the Principle of Passion came into my life before Purpose did. That's okay, because like I said, any one of these 7 Principles will change the direction of your life in a positive way. At the time, I didn't know about the other Principles. This book has come from me examining the totality of my transformation. If you find yourself gravitating to one Principle, then go ahead and explore that one further and allow it to be a catalyst into the others. Just don't let yourself get stuck to one. Allow yourself to be open to all of them. **Keep digging and exploring until you're applying all 7**. You'll start to feel a powerful sense of control when you do apply just one of them. That's nothing compared to the power you feel in your life when all 7 Principles are engaged!

So, to answer the question I set forth, there are perhaps different ways in which you may "find" your Purpose. Try using any of the other Principles to spark your engine. Your true Purpose may take some time for it to be fully revealed, just have some Patience (another Principle we will discuss in another chapter). There are some things you can do to get you in the right direction. I believe that once you find your purpose you'll know. It may have been in front of your face all along, like me, but once you find it, it will be obvious. Below is a poem I wrote that perfectly describes what I felt when I knew my purpose:

20/20

2020 is looking 20/20 to me.
The future is picture perfect as far as the eye can see.
My sight is super focused and I have no time
for hocus pocus.
Blurring out the fakeness centers me into reality.

Hi-definition is virtually stunning.
Three dimensions through my spectacles so I can see the truth spectacularly.
I'm viewing everything now in crystal clear clarity.
No more tripping over awkward feet while running,
my vision has me going forward at top speed and gunning.

Mind, body, and soul connected now.
Drug nor drink could never make me feel as good as I do now.
I finally know now what it's like to be truly healthy.
At a place of total peace and ultimate serenity.
In 2020 I'll be 40 with 20/20 vision looking like I'm 20.

--Joshua S. Kangley

I wrote that poem after I had discovered my purpose. I bet you can feel the level of confidence and enthusiasm I had for the future. Let me ask you, "What's your 20/20 vision for 2020?" You can start today and by 2020 you'll be surprised at how far you came.

Let's get down to the meat and potatoes of this chapter. I have sporadically hinted at how to apply the Principle of Purpose in your life, and hopefully, I have described how important it is and what it means. If it hasn't become clear yet, I want to show you a diagram that will put it all together visually. Then I will wrap up this chapter with things you can do to help put you in front of your Purpose and my advice to you on this subject.

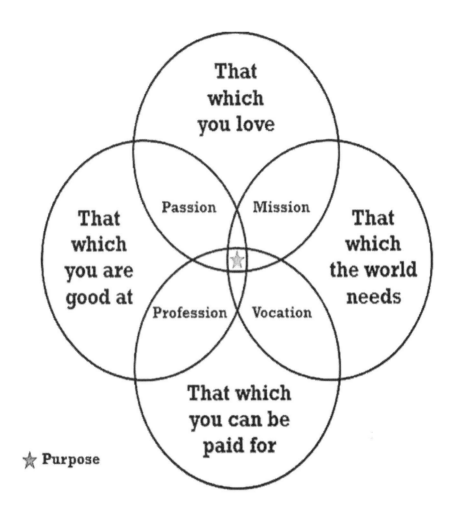

That
which
you love

Passion   Mission

That
which
you are
good at

That
which
the world
needs

Profession   Vocation

That which
you can be
paid for

☆ Purpose

As you can see, your Purpose is found smack dab in the middle of some things you're going to need to think about. Like I said, this may take some time if you're still living in a reactionary state. You'll need to navigate out of that fog I described earlier. Remember, I did it and so can you. I'm going to tell you what I did to clear my mind and get out of that negative state of mind, which led me to finding my Purpose.

Part 1. Balance Your Mind, Body, Soul or "Clearing"

The first step is to clear yourself so you can be in a state of mind to receive your true Purpose. We all have an intuition that we're born with. We know what's good for us and what's bad. When we do things that make us happy, that's our inner intuition speaking to us, saying, "This is good, keep doing things like this!" When we have a bad feeling about something, that's our inner intuition warning us, saying, "Whoa, this is not the direction to go!" The problem is, when we are living in a reactionary state, which most of us are in some degree or another because today's society has so many distractions and limitations, we're not navigating our lives to the full potential. We get caught up in a 9-5 mentality, we get caught up in the negative news cycle, we get caught into a routine and are blinded to the opportunities that are right in our face, sometimes. So how do we disconnect from all this and get centered? Here are some things you can do: Essentially, clearing, as I refer to it, means taking all negativity from within you and constantly replacing and cycling through positivity. Think of it this way: you're exactly what you put into your body—so you may as well make it good.

Mind

Read: Read self-help books like the one you're reading now or articles and magazines that can enrich your life or are about things you wish to learn more about. I have some recommendations which I will share at the end of the book, but there are many out there, get started.

TV/Devices: Try shutting it off for a while. Take a break from the negative news cycle. Get off the couch chilling all day with Netflix. I'm not asking you to throw the television away but take a break from the binging and all the negativity and use it to your advantage. If you do watch Netflix, try watching an inspiring documentary or movie. There are some good ones on there as I write this book. I'll give recommendations at the end of the book. Even on YouTube, you can find many motivational and inspirational videos, Ted Talks being one of them, that you can stream or watch on your device.

Radio/Music: Whether we admit it or not, the things we listen to, watch, and engage with influence our behavior and decisions in some capacity or another. If you're serious about success and achieving maximum results, you must be willing to make some changes. Listen to motivational talk radio instead of the news or negative music. Listen to inspiring audio books. Music is an important part of our lives and can be healing in many ways, just make sure it's music that has a good message and inspires you.

Meditate: Take some time to ponder in the stillness. Focus on nothing but your breathing. In the morning, right after waking, take some time before you start your day to be thankful for another day and think about what you hope to accomplish. At night, before you sleep, take a moment to be thankful for the day and all that you have. You can meditate anywhere. It's all about taking all the distractions away and calming the mind. I'm not an expert but you can easily search out different methods of meditation and choose what works for you.

Positive Affirmations: Get in the habit of thinking positive thoughts and saying to yourself, out loud, that you're worth it and that you have value. Again, I'm no expert, but you can search many positive affirmations. Go through them and find some that you like and give you the best results. Be sure to check out the end of the book for some of my favorites.

Body

Diet: Feeding your body food high in nutrition is very important. Your body needs fuel for energy and if you're powering your body with good food you're going to operate at a higher level and be able to go the distance. You're going to feel better and when you feel better, you're going to do better. There's been so much talk about nutrition, so many books, so many debates on food but it really isn't rocket science. Drink a lot of water, eat more fruits and vegetables, stay away from fast food as much as you can and that's really all you have to do. I know this sounds simple but it really comes down to eating more actual food that's nutritious, which is what our body wants, and less junk food. As simple as I think it is I understand for others it can be complex. You can do your own research very easily, and through that research, find a balance that works for you.

Exercise: Exercise is also important for your body. Now, I'm not saying you need to hit the gym every day and go crazy, but you should make an effort to get out, take walks, and do some running or bicycling. If you can't get outside, hit the treadmill or do anything you can to be active and get your body in motion. A body in motion stays in motion. Don't let yourself become idle and stationary, in other words—lazy.

Soul

Help Others: You can feed your soul happiness by helping others. There is nothing better than being able to help someone else. You can do this in many ways: by volunteering your time or donating items you no longer need. Find some way that you can give back to someone, even if it's just a friendly smile or holding the door. Anything, even the smallest act of kindness, can make a big difference and feed your soul.

Forgive/Ask Forgiveness: If there are things that are hanging you up, this is where it's time to clear it up. Forgiveness is all about taking weight off. If someone has wronged you in any way, forgive them in your heart. I'm not saying to necessarily forget or go on acting like it's all fine and dandy, but forgive that wrong doing, stop letting it tear you up inside and move on, for you. Forgiveness allows you to move on from being a victim. It takes all that weight off your shoulders. At the same time, if you have wronged someone, you need to ask forgiveness and come to a resolution, if possible. Express sorrow for what you have done and vow to be a better person.

Conversation: Seek out someone you trust or find interesting and just have a conversation. Go deeper than small talk and really get deep. Have an open mind to what the other person is saying and really listen to them. I challenge you to try this also with a complete stranger. Remember, be respectful and polite to their voice and genuinely be interested in what they're saying. Some of the most profound and life changing conversations I have had in my life were with complete strangers.

I understand that a lot of this may seem uncomfortable, especially if you're not used to some of these concepts. Most of us today are too stimulated or distracted by society. I mean, think about it. How easy do they make it for us to eat unhealthy foods, watch junk on the TV, become slaves to our devices, slaves of routine. It's so easy because it's everywhere, constantly being pushed down our throats and in our faces. If you can bear with me and have an open mind, and try to apply these into your life, it may not be easy—but it will damn sure be worth it. You're better than that and you deserve better. Also, I want to remind you that I'm not licensed in any way, professionally or otherwise to give any advice on diet or nutrition. I'm simply telling you what I have done that worked for me and I believe, through my own life experiences of close to 40 years now, that it will help you too. I encourage you to seek out and do your due diligence on what I'm relaying to you. Use the information I'm providing you to be the basis to get you engaged and start your journey to success.

Part 2. Self-Analysis

Okay so here is where we're going to put it all together and help you find your Purpose. Once you have put yourself in a state of balance and cleared out the junk in your life, you're ready to go on to part two, which is about self-exploration and evaluation. Here is where we examine ourselves, which we're now more prepared to do now that we have moved into a state of balance. This is where you're going to ask yourself a lot of questions and you may even be asking family and friends for feedback as well. Essentially, it's all about finding out who you are and what makes you happy and how you can use that to not only make money, but to help others and make a difference in the world. Here we go! These are some provoking questions to help you get started.

What beliefs and values do you hold dear? Why?

What type of person do you see yourself as? Why?

What's important in your life? Why?

What do others (ask family and friends) think about you? What do they say are your talents/gifts?

What are you really good at?

What do you really like to do? Why?

What do you really want to do? Why?

These are some fundamental questions you can start asking yourself. Have an open mind and allow yourself to be totally honest. There different ways of doing this. You can also list out all your talents and gifts (things you're really good at) and then make a list of things you like to do or are interested in. Then, make a list of what your family and friends say about you. Go through those lists and match up any similarities. Figure out how you can use that to make money and help others. Essentially, that's your purpose. Only you will know it and to only you will it be revealed. I know that this may seem simple. It's not, though. Remember how long it took me? However, it also doesn't have to be difficult. If I had these tools that I'm sharing with you, I believe I would have come to my Purpose a lot sooner. You can find your Purpose and be on your way to success in no time with these Principles. I encourage you to use the diagram and these questions to start provoking you into digging deep and really finding out who you are and what your Purpose is.

Let's Recap!

If you're reading this, then you already are on your way. The very fact that you picked up this book and are reading it tells me that you're serious about your success and happiness. I want to thank you and congratulate you on getting through the first Principle. The powerful Principle of Purpose. The diagram and the self-analysis questions will be a great start for you to explore this Principle and eventually find your Purpose—that's what the goal is here. As you read this book, I'd like you to keep a journal. Grab a notebook and use it solely in respect to this book. Take notes and jot down anything that comes to your mind. Write down ideas that pop up or thoughts you want to explore later. This will be a great tool for you because even though you may not know your Purpose after this chapter, I believe it will come to you by the end of the book. As you make notations or possibly when you go back through it, it will pop out at you—keep an open mind and heart. Here is what I believe are the important take-aways from this chapter on Purpose:

- Keep a journal (make notations as you read this book and write down thoughts and ideas)
- Get balanced or cleared (mind, body, soul)
- In your journal, make some lists
    - list all your talents/gifts (what you're really good at)
    - list all the things you like doing and what you're interested in
    - list attributions that your family and friends attach to you
    - describe how you see your ideal life
- Have an open mind and be receptive to new ideas and opportunities
- Practice living in a positive proactive state and let go of negativity
- Go over your lists and start thinking about the similarities and matches
- Use those similarities to begin to form what you believe your Purpose is

Remember, to find your Purpose, you must be living in a healthy balance. Put good things into your mind, body, and soul, practice the action of seeking out your true Purpose through self-analysis—and it will be revealed to you. Once you find it, don't let it go. Hold on to it and work on developing ways to live your life in your Purpose, on purpose. What you may find out may surprise you or maybe you knew deep down all along. Whatever it is, protect it from all naysayers and doubters because you'll be happier and more successful than anyone ever thought.

Principle 2:
Passion

"Passion is energy. Feel the power
that comes from focusing on what excites you."
--Oprah Winfrey

When talking about Passion, it's often referred to as a "thing". For example, you've heard the expression when asked, "What's your passion in life?" For me, however, Passion is an energy you live "with". It's more of a feeling and power than a "thing". I also believe that Passion is already inside all of us—it just needs to be released or awakened, or sometimes reawakened. So, when I refer to Passion in this chapter and throughout the book, I will be basing it on my interpretation of the word and what it means to me. I happen to agree with the Merriam-Webster Dictionary definition, which I believe is spot on:

4 b: intense, driving, or overmastering feeling or conviction

Once you have found and made a commitment to live in your Purpose, it needs to be driven by your Passion. Think of it this way—your Purpose is "what" you want and your Passion is your "why". If you're excited about your Purpose and your goals in life and on top of that, passionate about achieving them and realizing your true potential, it will drive you, day in and day out, keeping you in cruise mode on your path to success.

At the beginning of every year, millions of people get inspired by resolutions. It always starts off with great intentions for bettering ourselves. We say, "I will lose weight this year" or "I will spend more quality time with the family" or "I will travel more", etc. We all know what happens though, don't we? They don't last more a month. Why is this? I believe this happens because, although there are good intentions behind these resolutions, they're empty ones. **There is no Purpose to guide them and no Passion to drive them.** You see, most people are already caught up in the routine of their day-to-day life. People tend to, once they're comfortable, stick to what they know and what they were taught. So, when the end of the year comes along, it makes people suddenly examine themselves. *Where did the year go? Boy, time sure flew by! Uh oh, I better get on this* people will say to themselves. Most people are so wrapped up in their life that the year just passes them by and they are so surprised that the end of the year has come. So, January comes and it's a new year. Time for change, right? This end of the year phenomenon acts as a sudden urge to make a change for the better. However, January goes by and then it's back to the same old routine. This urge is brief. **Resolutions rarely ever stick because they are empty goals–without Purpose to guide them and Passion to drive them.**

This end of the year urge to examine ourselves and make the next year better is important to take a look at. It proves that we're capable of doing it. It proves that, at least once a year, we're willing to take some steps to better and enrich our lives in different ways. Imagine though, if we were able to keep the momentum going all year round. Imagine that the initial spark to change in January kept on going. Is it possible? I believe it's absolutely possible and that given the right tools, anyone can reach any goal they put their mind to. They just need a clear idea of their Purpose and live with Passion. These two powerful Principles can alone drive anyone to success. They must be followed up by the other Principles of Success that we will get to later, but they are so powerful that when used together nothing can stop you. Because any goal or goals you set for yourself, if you have Purpose to guide you and Passion to drive you, the only outcome is success. **Empty intentions, though they may be good, are no match for comfortability.** As days go on, without Purpose and Passion, we will retreat slowly back to old habits, and most of us eventually fail—

resolutions right into the trash bin. The ones who succeed have a Purpose and this Purpose is fueled by an intense desire—Passion. Passion is like a fire and you must keep it burning or it can go out. Remind yourself of your Purpose and why you started in the first place, focusing on the big Picture (another powerful Principle we will discuss in the last chapter).

In 2015, I found myself overweight and, to be honest with you, stuck on the couch way too often. I had become comfortable. Our business was doing fine, we had a healthy, active, and beautiful child, bills were getting paid, and we were living comfortably. Though I didn't know it at the time, comfortable can be a dangerous thing to be. It came to a shocking jolt one night when I woke up gasping for breath. It was a very scary feeling I will never forget. I had never really been a snorer, but at this point I had gained a lot of weight and developed sleep apnea. I had shortness of breath, and even just walking up the steps in our home was a strain. I also had chest pains and pressure that I had never experienced before and high blood pressure, all of which I chose to ignore, until that night. When I finally caught my breath, I was so worried about it that I made an immediate life-changing decision. It wasn't even a question. I started a diet the very next day and vowed to only eat very nutritious foods, like vegetables and fruits, and drink lots of water. I cut out all junk food and anything that wasn't rich in nutrients. On top of that, I got off the couch and became more active. I made my health a top priority and in just 30 days of doing this I lost about 50 pounds and was motivated to continue living a healthier lifestyle. I started to feel so great and had so much energy that I didn't want to be on the couch, and had no desire for junk food or fast food. This positive life change had ripple effects in all aspects of my life. I had this new-found energy that propelled me like never before. Little did I know it would be the catalyst in my life that would lead me to my Purpose.

I was feeling better than ever and I was acting in a proactive state. Remember, when you're in this state of living, opportunities and profound realizations come to you. Essentially, it's the Law of Attraction. The Law of Attraction has been discussed a lot in recent years especially with the movie, "The Secret." I do recommend that movie, more like a documentary of sorts, for you to watch. You'll need to watch it over and over again to understand the concepts they talk about and to let them sink in. Watch it with an open mind. For those of you who may not know what the Law of Attraction is, it's essentially this: what you put out, you attract back to you. Whatever you think about most will eventually manifest itself in some sort of physical way. Also, you can create the life you wish by thinking about it with a feeling of expectation or as if it already exists. I will talk a little bit more about this later in the book, but that's only a simplistic description about the Law of Attraction. I encourage you to explore more in depth for yourself, as there are plenty of resources that go into a deeper explanation. So, I was attracting more Positive opportunities and I was having revelations come to mind about myself and what I should be doing—my Purpose was coming into focus. Like I said before, each one of these Principles is very powerful on its own. I was applying Passion in my life and it drove me to a healthier lifestyle. It was propelling me to make better decisions and allowing me to see more Positive opportunities and bringing my Purpose into the light. So, you don't have to start with Purpose just because it's at the beginning of the book. Remember for me, I've used motivation or sense of urgency at least a couple of times to bring about Positive change in my life. Any one of the Principles, if applied in your life, will bring about Positive change. What is important is that you keep that Positive momentum by learning about and applying the other six Principles. **When you have all 7 Principles of Success actively applied in your life, your success is inevitable.**

Let's go back to when I was in jail. Remember, I said that immediately I knew I was never coming back and that I decided to straighten my life out right then and there. Well, I did that and that intense sense of urgency helped me straighten out my life. But, I never knew about the other Principles at that time so the momentum faded. I kept going on in life and eventually settled into routine and comfort. Later, when I used Passion again to get healthier and live a long time for my kids, I allowed myself to go even further and that's when I learned about Purpose. It's when my Purpose was coming together. Eventually, we sold the business that we loved and had run for several years and invested in another business that brought more income than we had seen in the whole time we had been together as a couple. We went from 30,000.00 generated revenue to 150,000.00 generated revenue, literally overnight. This all happened because of a shift in my attitude and a shift in my way of living. This is how powerful the Principle of Passion is. It can drive you like no other. I believe if you apply Passion in your life, you can experience his kind of change as well. You must be willing to have an open mind and to do things you haven't done before. You have probably heard the expression, "to achieve things you never have before, you must be willing to do things you never have before." This is 100% true. You have to think outside of the box and be willing to go for goals no matter what. This is where Passion comes in. It drives you to achieve and reach a level of success you haven't seen before. Not only that, it can lead you right into your Purpose. For me, I discovered, finally at the age of 36, that my Purpose is to help people by telling my story and helping at least one other person find their Purpose.

Remember, I said earlier that Passion is your "why". So, for me, my family was my "why" and motivated me, fueled me, to do whatever I needed to do to reach my goal of losing weight and living healthy. You need to have a sense of urgency and burning desire. Here is a quote that perfectly describes the Passion you need to possess to reach your goals:

"When you want to succeed as bad you want to breathe then you'll be successful"
--Eric Thomas

That sense of urgency came out of a grave concern for my health. It literally jolted me into action. I wanted to be around a long time for my daughter and to have more children as well. I wanted to teach them, guide them, and love them for as long as I could. Being here for my kids became something that motivated me to push me through all the tough times and keep me on track. I was living in a state of Passion. Now, I sincerely hope that this kind of jolt isn't what finally gets you started nor do I believe it to be a requirement for change. You can decide today to take control of your life and live your Purpose on Purpose and find ways to be inspired and live with Passion.

What is motivating you right now? I have a feeling there's a reason you're reading this book and if you've made it this far, you're serious about whatever your reasoning is. Consider that because I'm betting there's a motivating factor. Maybe you want more out of life? Maybe you haven't been able to get to the level of success you know is out there for you? Maybe you've been to jail or are in jail now? Maybe you're looking for some motivational tools? Maybe you're at a plateau in your career. Whatever it is, explore that a bit more and you'll find that you already have Passion inside you. We need to get that out and released and we need to use that to drive us. Don't let yourself become another good-intentioned person with resolutions only to have them end up in the trash a few weeks later. You need to discover your Passion and let that drive you while your Purpose guides you. If you haven't discovered either of them yet, have Patience (another Principle we will talk about later) and it will come to you.

Let's Recap!

- Purpose is your "what" and Passion is your "why"
- Your Purpose guides you while your Passion drives you
- Keep your eyes on the prize or the big Picture!

- Passion is the underlying force or energy that's driving you towards your Purpose
- Dig into what motivates you. (You may be able to find your Purpose AND Passion with this exercise!)
    - Is it your family?
    - Is it to have a better job or own your own business?
    - Is it to be healthier or lose weight?
    - Is it to help other people?
    - Is it to be connected more to people?

Principle 3:
Positivity

(Now, before we begin, I'm in no way saying that just thinking positive is all you ever have to do. I'm not saying that if you think good thoughts, suddenly the pain is going to go away or that it will make obstacles disappear. Not at all. However, I know the value of positive thinking and I know from my own experience that it can change your life. Have an open mind as you read this chapter and I'm sure there is something here that will grab you.)

This is my favorite Principle to talk about! That's not to say that it's the only Principle I follow, nor the only one I suggest you solely pay attention to. I've said it before, all 7 Principles are important and powerful in each one's own right. If you can apply just one of them, you're going to be seeing awesome changes. If you can apply all 7, you're going to be unstoppable! I'm just a very Positive person. I haven't always been this way, but these days, regardless of any negative thing that happens, I tend to try and find the Positive or flip it into a Positive. Living in this state of mind is way less stressful and I believe you'll find many more happy and Positive experiences. Remember**, like attracts like**. If you go around feeling angry and resentful you're going to attract that back to you. Let's be honest, who wants to be around someone who is angry and resentful? I used to walk through life this way myself. I was hurt and that hurt led to me being angry. I started living in a reactionary and defensive state of mind. When I learned about Positivity, I changed my way of thinking and lived in a proactive and Positive way. I let go of some very difficult things. I forgave the people who hurt me. I didn't forget, and trust me, some of those people I will never be around again. But for me, I let it go and I chose to forgive. There is a tremendous power in Positivity and it's something that you can practice immediately and see immediate results. Positive thinking is a widely talked about subject and there are many naysayers about it. These critics call it too idealistic or too unrealistic, too corny, too simplistic, crazy, a bunch of fluff, etc. However, I'm here to tell you that **there's real power in the way you think and in the thoughts you harbor in your mind.** The question for you is, would you rather have that power work in your favor in a positive way or against you in a negative way?

The Principle of Positivity doesn't suggest living in Positivity equals never having negative emotions. We are human beings and we all experience emotions like hurt, sorrow, disappointment, etc. That's normal. We're allowed to acknowledge these feelings and emotions. In fact, they could be healing, but do not dwell and live in them. Let then come and let them go. If you feel sad, let it come, embrace it and accept it. If tears flow, let them, and then breathe and let it go. Let it pass you like a wind, in and then out. Move on as soon as you can. It's okay to look back and reflect, for there's a possibility of learning from the situation or even seeing a Positive side to it. Now, I know that seems hard and maybe impossible. For instance, God forbid, you lose someone you love very much. This, of course, is heartbreaking, incredibly sad and painful. Let those feelings and emotions come. They will hit you hard, it's part of our humanity. Accept the loss when you're ready, then let it go. Don't let their memory go, but the pain. Reflect and be thankful that you had someone so special that you loved and that you had their love. Understand that you're better for having known that person and appreciate the life they lived and the life you still have. Perhaps it makes you realize how important time is and to spend it wisely and strive to achieve great things before it's your time. Maybe, in their honor, you could embrace the qualities or aspects about him or her that you loved so much. This example is a difficult one. Death is always the hardest to talk about, but it's a part of our life and it doesn't have to be a negative thing. We should value life and the life we choose to live. Life is a cycle, we come and go. If we embrace death as a part of life's beautiful cycle, we can be less fearful of it and perhaps even enjoy life and living even more. Again, I know this is a tough subject and maybe raw for some readers. Please know that in no way, do I mean any disrespect nor am I suggesting that we shouldn't mourn. I don't mean to come across as cold and not understanding. Not at all. I have seen people unable to come to grips with difficult situations, like death, and not be able to move on. It's like it immobilizes them from living their own life. If we dwell in negative emotions for too long, it can be devastating. It keeps you from living and reaching success.

I'm sure most of us have experienced someone cutting you off while driving. This is an upsetting situation, right? Or, how about being stuck in traffic? Just driving to the store these days you may experience several of these traffic annoyances. So much so, that some people develop a thing called road rage. Stick with me here. Now, if you take a closer look at these road ragers, I'm betting they're very negative-minded people. I'm also betting that they're the type of people who are always grumpy, always complaining, and always angry. Either that or they're carrying some huge and heavy baggage inside and have a deep-seeded issue. That weight is negativity. Those issues are negativity. They have been carrying it for years, maybe not even fully realizing it. When you harbor negativity, it will eventually manifest itself. It will control your thoughts and your decisions in negative ways. It's also like a sort of cycle. If you have not released negativity in your life, it consumes you. You become that person in traffic who is "road raging." I'm guessing their life is one negative situation after another. They get stuck in every red light, something breaks down, they have bad relationships, they get fired, they spill coffee on themselves, etc. Their life is one big continuous negative situation, like the falling of dominoes. Instead of analyzing themselves and doing some self-help, they blame everything on everyone else and take no ownership or responsibility in their life. My point is, these people dwell on the situation and let it affect how they feel. They get consumed by negativity and it snowballs into every aspect of their life. If this is you, have no worries. I'm not judging you. In fact, thank you for reading this book as I believe you came to the right place. Please read on with an open mind and something is sure to stick out that will help you. If you're serious about big success, you're going to need to learn to let go and go with the flow, and start thinking more positively. So, instead of getting mad at the red light, the jerk who cut you off, or being stuck in traffic, let it go, and decide not to get caught up in something you can't control. If you catch yourself getting annoyed (who wouldn't?), just let it come. Accept it, breathe, and let go. Move on quickly. Then, if you can, challenge yourself to see the positive. If you're stuck in traffic, maybe you get more time to listen to some awesome music or that motivational audio book you just bought. Maybe, you get more time to mentally go over your notes for your meeting or drink some of your gourmet coffee you bought? Or, maybe, just maybe, divine intervention played a role? It's all about perspective. Now, I know this is a lot to sort through and I will talk more specifically about what you can do to help you think more positive later in the chapter. I just want you to begin to see how the way you're thinking can affect your life. Be optimistic in knowing you can take control of your thoughts and live a more proactive, Positive way that will direct you towards success.

I talked briefly earlier in the book about the Law of Attraction. Many of you have seen the movie "The Secret" or have read the book. If you haven't, you really should. It really put it all together very well. Essentially, "The Secret" is the Law of Attraction. Your thoughts become things. In other words, what you think about or obsess about manifests itself in the physical realm. So, you can literally create the life you want by thinking about it. Stay with me on this. I'm going to explain the best I can in my own words, but I do recommend doing your own research on the Law of Attraction.

Imagine this: on your way to work, you get stuck in traffic. You get upset because now you're going to be late for work. You start to dwell on this and now you're steamed. *Your facial expression has changed and so has your mood, from good to bad. You're upset and frustrated and you have let this consume you. You start to make aggressive driving maneuvers to try and beat the clock, because you are NOT going to be late. Another traffic light is turning red and because you have been speeding you have to hit the brake. The coffee you just bought at the drive-thru goes flying and spills all over your car. Now you're pissed and once the light turns green you hit the gas. The pressure is building inside you. At this point you're now about a block away from work when you hear sirens. In your rearview mirror, you see the flashing lights. You've now been pulled over and are really going to be late. The cop talks to you through your window and lets you know you were speeding. Now you have a ticket and are beyond pissed. By the time you get to work, your coffee is splattered all over the dash board of your car, you've gotten a speeding ticket, AND you're very late. You have tipped the scales of anger and frustration and are in total reactionary defensive mode. Your whole body is tense and your energy radiates what you're feeling inside. At work, co-workers try and say "hi" but because you're caught up in your anger, you don't seem very friendly. New employees, from their perspective, are getting this as a first impression and may choose to not approach you. Now, customers are complaining about you and the manager has to speak with you in her office about it.*

Do you see how this has all snowballed and that how you act or react to situations can change your interactions in life? This is how some of us actually live and this has happened to many people, unfortunately. You can see the destruction and cycle this can create if you're constantly living in this state of mind. Again, if you can relate to this I'm not judging you. I used to be like this. In fact, this situation isn't too far from being an example of situations I've been in. I used to be angry all the time. I used to be a "road rager" and negative. It landed me in jail. It kept me from growing earlier on in my life. It kept me from realizing my Purpose. Yet, I was able to change and shed all that negativity and live a positive life. If I can do it, you can too! I believe in you. If you're not sure, just be Patient and continue reading with an open mind. In addition, if you can't relate to any of that, then, like I said before, this can help you as well. You can see what CAN happen and you can be proactive and use these ideas to apply to your life to help you reach success.

Okay, so moving on. Now we can see what CAN happen when you let yourself be overcome with anger and negativity.

Notice how the co-workers and customers reacted to your energy in the first example. How would you react or feel around someone who acted like that? The thoughts in the example story manifested in the actions and in the physical world. Let's look at the opposite example next:

Imagine waking up from a full night's rest. You're feeling refreshed and fully awake, ready to start the day. You give thanks for the day and feel excited for the opportunities that may come your way. Not only are you excited for the opportunities that may come your way, but you expect them to come today! You expect your day to be filled with positivity and happiness. You give your wife a kiss good morning and go hug your kids who are also ready for a great day. On the way to work, you enjoy an audiobook on success and positivity. You gain new insight and are thankful for that and can't wait to apply it in your life. You let people who are in a hurry pass you and cut in front of you because you're not worked up about how it makes you feel. In fact, it makes you feel good to be helpful and nice to others. After all, you're not in a hurry because you anticipated heavy traffic and left a bit earlier so you would have plenty of time. Plus, it gives you more time to ponder over what you have just learned on your audiobook and drink your coffee before you get to work. Once, you get to work you're happy and ready to be productive. Your whole being has a positive energy about it and it radiates off you. You're smiling and it's contagious. As you pass people and greet them, they can't help but smile back at you. Your smile has made them feel good also. Customers love you and they are making compliments. Soon, the manager wants to see you.

What do you think the manager wants to see you about in this example? A raise? Promotion? I would imagine it's a very different reason than the one in the first example. Believe it or not, both examples are from my own life. I used to be like the first one and those things happened to me. Now, I live just like the second one. So, now you see how different those examples are and how it's possible to turn it around. You see, **whether you're thinking positively or negatively, you're creating energy**. Your thoughts, if they make you feel good, will produce good energy, and if they're negative, bad energy. And people can pick up on this energy. We are essentially all energy and we can tune in and pick up on other people's energy through their behavior. We have the power, by thinking positive and using positive energy to create a positive life for ourselves. This is the Law of Attraction.

"All that we are is a result of what we have thought."
--Buddha

As I have mentioned before, I came from a very rough childhood. I don't want to go into detail out of respect to my family and because I really want to stay on topic. Perhaps that's a whole other book. It's all about the right time and right place. I want this book to be all about you and how you can apply these Principles. I love my parents and my family and I have come to an understanding of it all. That said, it is what it is. My childhood was rough and I experienced some traumatic things that affected me throughout my life. I should be able to talk about that and be open and honest in my feelings. However, I do not want to come across as blaming the adults in my life for everything that has gone wrong. Even though I do not blame them for me going to jail as I made the decisions that put me there, what does have to be understood is that I was influenced greatly by what I saw and what happened during my childhood.

So, I lived with this rage and anger and made bad decisions in my early life that landed me in jail. Remember, I described it earlier in the book as a fog or like I was living in a reactionary state of mind. People, like my pastor, were trying to warn me and get me out of this fog, but I was so uncontrollable that I couldn't hear or see what good-hearted people were trying to tell me. It was when I got to jail that reality set in and I was suddenly at the lowest of lows. It was a shock to my system and I knew I didn't belong there and I never wanted to come back. I accepted my punishment and did my time. I gave no excuses then and I don't now. I put myself there and I did my time. That was when I was 18 years old. Since then, I have completely turned my life around and made it my personal vow to never break the law again in any way. That vow sparked an incredible Passion and I was able to accomplish great things after I got out. It led me to living more Positively and to make Positive decisions. I surprised many people and even myself. I was at my bottom and I made the decision to pick myself up, and I never look back. How did I do it? How did I go from being in jail to success? Well, to put it simply, I changed my way of thinking. I made better choices for myself and cut off all ties with bad people I used to associate with. It wasn't easy but I knew it had to be done if I was going to live up to my promise. I traveled. I had to get my head clear and the best way to do it sometimes is to travel. I also read a lot of books. Especially motivational and inspirational self-help books. I did some serious self-analysis and discovery. I had to figure it all out on my own and it took a while, but I did it. I was at peace and went from reacting in a negative way to **proactively choosing to be Positive and not only allow Positivity in my life but to expect it**.

Your life experiences do not have to be like mine for you to have great change. In fact, I hope not. My Purpose is to tell you my story and prove to you that no matter where you are in life and what your background is, you can turn it around and live a life with more success and happiness. And yes, if you come from terrible circumstances, you can too. Read this book with an open mind at least twice and I believe in your ability to make it happen. You just need to decide to start today! So, I hope by now you can see the snowball effect that can happen when you dwell too long in negativity. Also, how you can use the snowball effect to your advantage by being proactive and choosing to be Positive. This may seem uncomfortable at first, so if you have to fake it until you make it, go ahead. Force yourself to smile right now and I bet you'll instantly feel a little better. Keep forcing a smile until you're always smiling! The negative snowball effect can also plow through generations. I have two daughters now and I'm so glad that I decided to stop the cycle in my life, otherwise I could easily be doing the same thing to them. We must make conscious decisions to make sure that we're not putting our baggage onto our kids. This could lead them into adulthood living resentful, destructive, and negative lives. I encourage you to stop the cycle of negative thoughts and add more Positivity in your life.

Tips to Help You Become More Positive:

- Live in the present.
- Be thankful for what you have already and where you are now.
- Focus on the Positive aspects of people or situations.
- Smile, smile, smile.
- Accept where you are now and know that you possess the tools to get where you want to be.
- Make a conscious effort to not allow negative thoughts to penetrate your mind.
- Turn off negative music, news, etc.
- Recite Positive affirmations to yourself.
- Get regular full nights of sleep.
- Wake up excited about your day.
- Expect opportunity and Positivity.
- Help others/perform random acts of kindness.
- Visualize and live in the feeling of the life you want as if you already have achieved it.

Let's Recap:

The reason I love this Principle so much is that it's fun to apply and you can see immediate results. In fact, if I were to suggest how to go about starting to apply the 7 Principles of Success, I would say start with Positivity. All it takes is a conscious decision to be positive. I would argue it takes more energy to be negative and angry all the time. Nobody wants that. So, if you're going to be anything, be Positive. This is key for your journey to success. If you start applying Positivity in your life, you'll be amazed at how rapidly things start changing. I know it can be difficult, especially if there are deep underlying issues in a person's life. Just thinking positive is not going to cure major mental issues, but the power of Positivity can make all the difference.

It all comes down to attitude and how you choose to go about life. I encourage you to work on finding ways you can be more positive. You're going to feel better and happier and other people around you will see you as someone who's very approachable. It's almost as if you have a glow and it's contagious.

The Two Best Ways to Become More Positive:

The fastest and best way to feel more Positive and get yourself into this mindset is to be genuinely thankful for what you already have. Maybe you don't have much, at least that's what you might think. But, if you take a moment, you'll begin to realize you have a lot. If you're reading this book, you can be thankful for any insight you obtain. You can be thankful for your health. You can be thankful for your family, friends, and loved ones that inspire and care about you. There are so many things to be thankful for. Stop comparing yourself to others and be thankful. Appreciate where you are now and realize that even though you may not be exactly where you want to be, you're working on it and be confident in your ability to reach success. Having this mindset will put you on a path of Positivity. Another way is to help others in any way that you can. Volunteering your abilities, even if it's just your time, makes you feel better, and it helps you realize that you have a lot to be Positive about.

Principle 4:
Planning

"People with goals succeed because they know where they're going."
--Earl Nightingale

When you have your Purpose realized to you and you decide to live in your Purpose on purpose, when you've unleashed your Passion inside, and when you've committed yourself to having a Positive mindset—you're now at the point where you can get these ideas formulated on paper and start Planning your path to success. This is where the rubber meets the road, so to speak. It's time now to take these ideas you've been having and write down a concrete Plan to help you reach your success. Planning is extremely important because it's in the planning stage when things get serious. Think of yourself like a military strategist meticulously Planning an operation that's going to make your goals a reality. When you're Planning, have the confidence that your Plan is going to work and you have the tools, resources, and mindset to organize a Plan that will put you directly on the path to success. **This is your Purpose in action**.

Now, what I'm about to say next might seem contradictory. Yes, Planning is important and powerful and you need to set Specific, Measurable, Achievable, Realistic, and Time-Based goals (known as S.M.A.R.T. goals). However, I don't want to get caught up in the specifics of how to Plan. There are many resources out there that go in depth on how to Plan and set goals. I believe that people can get too involved in this process and spend too much time writing and Planning, instead of taking action. So, my advice to you is to write out your goals, exactly what you want to achieve—and then set out to do it. Don't get me wrong, Planning is very important, but equally so is action, and it must directly follow—otherwise it will be just another Plan. Moreover, I believe that once you have your Purpose, and you're inspired by Passion and Positivity, your goals will come to you rather quickly. By now, I'm sure you already have a sound idea on the direction you want to take. Your path to success is becoming clearer. **Formulate your plan and then get to action.**

"In preparing for battle, I have always found that plans are useless but planning is indispensable."
--Dwight D. Eisenhower

For me, it's very important that you write out your goals and then write down the steps you think are going to help you achieve them. Setting a definite time will push you to reach them and give you accountability. I'm sure many you have heard or seen the acronym, S.M.A.R.T. Goals, (Smart, Measurable, Achievable, Realistic, Time-Based). If not, I will explain a little bit. I believe, when it comes to writing goals, this acronym perfectly describes how it should be done. It first appeared in 1981, in an edition of Management Review. The title was, "There's a S.M.A.R.T. way to write management goals and objectives." It was written by George Doran, Arthur Miller, and James Cunningham. It has caught on since then and has become a popular way to look at goals. I consider it the only way to approach goal writing and I recommend using it.

S.   Specific   *(What **exactly** will you do?)*

| M. | Measurable | *(How will you know if you **meet** your goal?)* |

M. Measurable *(How will you know if you **meet** your goal?)*

A. Achievable *(What **steps** are you going to take to reach your goal?)*

R. Realistic *(Can you achieve this goal? **How** likely?)*

T. Time-Based *(**When** do you want to complete your goal?)*

Let's Recap!

Planning is everything! However, Plans are only just Plans. You need to follow through and act on your Plans. What Planning does is prepare you for battle. It gives you guidance, like a road map, to navigate through your life and be able to reach success. Planning is only part of the equation. To keep the momentum going, you must have a Positive mindset and Passion to drive you with Purpose. You can have the best laid out plans, but if you're not motivated to act, they will just sit there, waiting.

I encourage you to use the S.M.A.R.T. acronym and get started writing out your goals and Planning your success. This Principle has power on its own, as each individual Principle contains unique power, so you'll see some Positive results and you'll be well on your way. Make sure to apply techniques to have all 7 Principles of Success firing in unison to maximize your results.

I can't say this enough—don't get too caught up in the Planning stage. Sometimes, Plans change. The goals and the big Picture will always stay the same, but as you get into the battle, your Planning will have prepared you. But the plans themselves, or actions, may change to conquer your goals. And that's totally okay. Constantly adjust your Plans to make your actions more efficient. There's real power in the confidence you'll have when you see your goals laid out and organized into a plan. It makes your vision concrete and gives you a path to navigate.

Principle 5: Persistence

Michael Jordan was cut from his varsity high school basketball team. Yes, that's right, you read it correctly. He, like all other successful people, used that experience to motivate him to up his game and try again the next year. He didn't let that "failure" discourage him. It might have made others quit trying or lose all hope, but not Jordan. Not only did he make the team the very next year, he became the star player, and after that, the rest is history. Michael Jordan is still considered that greatest NBA of all time.

"I've missed more than 9,000 shots in my career. I've lost almost 300 games. 26 times, I've been trusted to take the game winning shot and missed. I've failed over and over and over again in my life. And that is why I succeed."

--Michael Jordan

There's story after story like that of Michael Jordan, of ordinary people who achieve the extraordinary because of the power of Persistence. They achieve success beyond anyone's imagination except for their own. Because inside, they knew they would be successful at what they were setting out to do. They saw themselves winning and lived in that feeling. There's no greater story that perfectly describes the power of this Principle than that of Thomas Edison. Here was a boy whose teachers said "was too stupid to learn anything." He was fired from his first two jobs for being "non-productive". As an inventor, Edison made 1,000 unsuccessful attempts at inventing the light bulb. When a reporter asked, "How did it feel to fail 1,000 times?" Edison replied, "I didn't fail 1,000 times. The light bulb was an invention with 1,000 steps." Can you see the similar perspectives that Michael Jordan and Thomas Edison both shared? They never gave up. They didn't look at them as failures, instead they looked at them as lessons or steps that helped them to achieve massive success. It's all about perspective. **The power of Persistence will help you overcome "failures" and avoid giving up**. Imagine if Edison gave up at the 999th "fail?" He never would have reached his goal of inventing the light bulb and perhaps someone else would have. What if Jordan gave up basketball after being initially cut from the team? Can anyone imagine the NBA without Jordan? These men persisted in the face of all odds and kept on going. They did not give up. They doubled down and went for it. They learned from all the mistakes and "failures" and honed their craft and produced better and better results. This is what you must do to achieve success in your life. You must Persist in the pursuit of your goal and believe that you can reach it and WILL reach it, even if others don't. Know your Purpose, be Passionate about it and what you love to do, and live in a Positive mental state while you Plan your success. Feel excited about taking power into your own hands as you create the life you deserve. Get inspired by doing what you love and helping others. Start seeing yourself as already the person you want to become. Live in the feeling of having accomplished your goal, for it's right around the corner. Then, be Persistent and never, never, never, give up.

A few years ago, I submitted a manuscript of poetry to a poetry chapbook contest. I've been writing poetry since about the age of 13, but only recently felt brave enough to share my work and submit it to literary magazines and journals. My manuscript was rejected. I was almost feeling totally discouraged when I decided to turn it around and was determined to win the next year. You see how I didn't let myself stay in that negative feeling? If I had, I would have given up writing poetry, thinking I wasn't good enough. I didn't give up, though. Instead, for a whole year, I worked on my manuscript. I dug deeper and revised it over and over again. I wrote on a piece of paper, "I will win the contest!" I saw myself turning in my very best work and winning. I changed some poems, took some out, and wrote some new ones that fit into the manuscript better—right up to the due date. I felt it was a complete body of work that best represented my skills and was happy about it. I knew it would win. And guess what? Sure enough, a few months later, I received an email form the editor saying I won. That experience showed me the important of Persistence and the power it has. Believe in yourself. Success is not an easy ladder to climb. **The path to success will have its challenges and you need to Persist and never give up**. Turn those rejections into learning lessons. Turn "failures" into steps towards success. Take a look at some other people, like you and me, who have taken a "failure" or setback and used it to motivate them to achieve success.

Ordinary People Who Achieved Extraordinary Success by Being Extraordinarily Persistent

- Oprah Winfrey was fired because her emotion was not good for television broadcasting.

- Albert Einstein didn't speak until the age of four, didn't read until age seven, and was expelled from school.

- Walt Disney was fired for apparently having a lack of imagination.

- <u>Elvis Presley</u> was told not to pursue a singing career and that he should go back to his day job, which was a truck driver.

- <u>Abraham Lincoln</u> was demoted in the military, failed at many businesses he tried to start up, and lost several runs for office before he became President.

Let's Recap!

There's just one simple thing to know: there's no such thing as failure. It's all about perspective. If you have a goal you want to reach more than anything, you need to give it all you got. Have enough respect for your goal to keep going and no matter what anyone says, if it's important to you, do not give up. "Failures" are learning lessons and remember, anyone who's been successful has failed more times than you can imagine. Change your perspective, change your life. Ordinary people, with extraordinary Persistence, will always achieve extraordinary success.

Principle 6:
Patience

We come to Patience. Patience does not mean idleness or procrastination. You can't sit on the couch and say, "I'm being Patient." You can't wait for success to come to you. In this book, I speak about Patience as being calm and centered, with peace in your mind that what you're doing, your actions, are leading you to success. I speak of Patience as a confidence. This peace of mind or inner confidence will help you along your journey. Once you start living in your Purpose, many opportunities and things you've never been aware of will begin to pop up. You'll need Patience, not only in the overall process of your journey, but more specifically in making decisions on those opportunities. When you're absolutely living in true Purpose with Positivity and Passion, the right opportunities will come your way and the best ones for you will make themselves known. I believe you'll feel it in your heart and soul. Look at Edison again, he knew what he wanted. He was absolutely sure about his ability, but he was Patient with himself and the process, which allowed him to get through 1,000 "fails." So, for me, Patience is the ability to let life happen, or the process happen, and to be confident in your new-found attitude to be proactive rather than reactive to what life brings, and make the right decisions. Patience gives you power. You're in control of your emotions and not making rash decisions. It gives you peace and inner calm. In a sense, you're harnessing your energy and using it in a Positive way to guide you through life and reach your success. That's something to feel good about.

I know this is probably a lot to digest, but in short, the Principle of Patience is to simply TRUST. Trust in the process, trust in yourself, and in your instincts. Be Patient and calm and know that, indeed, you're on your way to success. Great things are about to happen any moment for you, they're already on the way. Don't let yourself live in a negative reactionary state of mind. Instead, live in a Positive, proactive state to make actions that keep you on a momentum towards your goals. Patience is power. So, if you're seeing a shift in your life, are starting to get excited about unleashing the power within you, are ready to start living your Purpose and reach success no matter where you are at in life, then go out and set forth on your journey. Be patient and live with that power and you'll be happier and more successful in all areas of your life.

By this time, you should now have a direction to which your inner compass is pointed. If you have really done the work, soul searched, and decided to go confidently in the direction of your true Purpose, you're on your way. You may even have already noticed opportunities coming your way or may have always been there, and are seeing things clearly because you're living in Purpose, on purpose. At, the very least, you have a good start to changing your life and have some tools to help you put yourself on the course to success. If, however, you're having trouble putting all this together, don't be discouraged. The mere fact you're reading this is a sign that you're determined to reach your goals and better your life. I believe in you and your ability and you should too. Most people don't make the effort to better themselves or to take steps towards their true self. The idea alone could be too intense and scary for most to make the leap of faith. Instead, they go through life stuck in a routine and that fog of comfortability. Most are stuck in a cycle of their own mental limitations and never dare to break through that. So, please, do not be discouraged. You're ahead of these people. This change may seem hard on the surface, but once you're living in your true Purpose, it's actually easier than you think and happier than you can imagine. My short, humble book is meant to be a basic starter kit of information based on my life and perception. I have years of experience and put this together for you, the reader, who is looking for inspiration. Ultimately, it will take your initiative and action to see yourself to the finish line. I encourage you to look at the additional resources I provide at the end of the book to give you a fuller perspective and idea of what I'm talking about. To be honest, information that's described in another book may explain it more eloquently than I can, or maybe you can relate to it better. I want to make sure that you fully understand each of the 7 Principles of Success, so if further reading is necessary, then I'm all for it. That said, I feel like each of these Principles are the TRUE Principles of Success and that if you understand them and apply them in your life, you'll find tremendous success. Don't make it more difficult than it needs to be. Do your due diligence in reading this book with an open mind and make the decision to apply each Principle in your life with a Positive attitude. **Remember, any motion going forward is still progress**. You must come to a point in your life when you make the decision to change and act on it. Any action you do take, in the pursuit of your goal, is going to set you up for success. **Consistent action, big or small, leads to eventual success**. So, go for it!

Let's Recap!

Remember, Patience is power! Having Patience puts you in control of your life. Because you're confident in your Purpose, you know that success is around the corner and opportunities are all around you. It gives control in making your decisions and choosing which opportunities to capitalize on in the efficiency of reaching your goal. Have Patience in this process. Be Patient with yourself. Be calm and live in the moment. Have the big Picture in your mind and work confidently towards that. I believe in you! Believe in yourself too!

Principle 7:
Big Picture

"I liked his ability to deal with a lot of negativity that surrounded him.
Even though he was in a world that he didn't want to be in,
he still saw the bigger picture."
--Dwayne Johnson

I've talked briefly a few times throughout this book about the big Picture. The big Picture is your end game, your goal, it's where you want to be—your vision. How you get to your big Picture or the navigation by which you pursue it may change. When you're on the battle field of success, the Plans you initially had may be thrown out or revised, but all that Planning has prepared and sharpened your mind. You know the terrain better than anyone and you're prepared to make your goal a reality, because you're focused—your eyes are on the prize. **The big Picture always stays the same.** You want to get a better job, you want to move out of the neighborhood to somewhere with more opportunity, you want to start a business, you want to finish school with high grades, you want to travel, etc. Those are the big Pictures. Everyone's is different. Don't let negative energy distract you from heading towards yours.

I suggest writing your big Picture on a big poster board and hang it somewhere in your home where you'll see it every day. I want that to get into your brain so it stays there and never leaves. So that when the challenges do come, and they will, you'll be reminded why you started this, and your eyes will remain on the prize. Having a big Picture state of mind helps you realize what's important and easily allows you to bypass negativity or something that's a waste of your time. If it's not helping you get to your end game, it's hurting you. For example, let's say there's a student named Joe studying for an exam the next day. This test is important because it accounts for a large portion of his grade in that class. He needs to get his grades up overall and doing well on this test will definitely improve his scores. He has a vision of graduating with honors. His buddies, however, want to go to this really cool house party and they're trying to convince Joe to go. Joe knows that every point counts and he is so close to his vision. What should Joe do? Our friend Joe, in this example, is strong-willed and he really is focused on his grades. He chooses to spend the night studying and getting prepared for the test. How well do you think Joe did? How well do you think his friends did? That's the power of the big Picture. When you have the big Picture mindset you can easily make important decisions that will put you closer and closer to your goals. Life happens, as we all know. We all have good intentioned friends who want us to party, we all work with difficult people, we all have family who may not be as supportive of us as much as we would like, this is life, and it's mostly unpredictable. However, your big Picture keeps you focused and on track. What matters in life is how we react to it, and better yet, how we proactively decide to act. **The big Picture mentality allows you to act on your life, to act on your Purpose.**

At this time, you have discovered your Purpose or are actively seeking out your Purpose. Remember, your Purpose is your true self, and this can take some time. It will require some self-discovery, breaking down walls, and really being courageous enough to analyze yourself. If you have never done this it could take some time, but you're well on your way and you're making the right decision. Keep an open mind and you'll see. Also, by now, you're living in Passion. You're Passionate about life, about making a change, about success, about your Purpose. You've also begun to live in a more positive state of mind by seeing the good instead of the bad in all people and situations. You've found yourself smiling more and people are interested in your change. You've been doing some planning about how you see yourself, what you hope to accomplish and how you'll do it. You've committed yourself to persist and never give up in the pursuit of your goals. You're feeling ready to take on the world. You're confident enough now to have patience and go forward making the best decisions for yourself that will get you closer to your goals. And now, you have your big Picture. You know exactly what you want and it's in your head. You're determined to keep your eyes on the prize until you reach it. You, my friend, are ready. You're ready to take this basic knowledge of the Principles I have laid out and ready to live the life you deserve, I believe in you and your abilities to accomplish things that maybe you thought never possible before. However, I bet by now you're starting to see it was possible all along. If I can do it, I know you can too, no matter where you're at in life. My best wishes to you and to all your successes!

Let's Recap!

The big Picture is the reason for your Purpose. It helps you focus and keeps your eyes on the prize. It also helps you easily choose actions that are in your best interest, keeping you on track. Think of this big Picture as your overall vision of your life, or your masterpiece painting of your life. Make your masterpiece a beautiful and epic mural of how you see yourself and the life that makes you happy.

Epilogue

This book is not meant to give you all the answers. It does provide the tools you'll need (the Principles), but the truth is, you have the answers. What I can promise you though is this: the 7 Principles of Success in this book are the very ones I used to reach my success. I was able, through the power of these key Principles, to turn my life around and go from jail (the bottom of the bottom) to success in all areas of my life. I was indeed very troubled, and if I can do it, I know that you can too! It was a hard road for me and I hope that's not the case for you. You can use these Principles no matter where you are in life. If you have found yourself at the bottom or if you come from a rough background, I want to tell you that **YOU** can bring yourself back up. That you **CAN** find your true Purpose and live a happier and more successful life. If you use these Principles in your life, you'll open yourself up to opportunities that you never thought possible. It's up to you, though, to make that commitment for change. Remember, I'm not a professional when it comes to psychology, financial advice, or any kind of counseling. I'm not licensed in any of these areas. So, as with anything, do your due diligence and explore on your own all the concepts I talk about. Consult a professional if you think it's necessary. However, I come to you with my experience and my years of personal exploration and self-improvement, and I hope that through sharing a little about my experience and how the 7 Principles changed my life, it will help you reach success in your life. I want to thank you for your time in reading this book. You should also be proud of yourself for taking the initiative and the first steps in making your life the life you deserve.

The Awesomeness Continues!

More Awesome Quotes:

"Live the life you have imagined." –Henry David Thoreau

"When things go wrong, don't go with them." –Elvis Presley

"In order to carry a positive action, we must develop here, (brain) a positive vision."
 –Dalai Lama

"What things you desire, when ye pray, believe that ye receive them, and ye shall have them."
–Mark 11:24

"Whatever the mind can conceive and believe, it can achieve." –Napoleon Hill

"Whether you think you can or think you can't, either way—you are right." –Henry Ford

"Life, is 10% what happens to me and 90% how I react to it." –Charles R. Swindoll

"By failing to prepare, you are preparing to fail." –Benjamin Franklin

"A goal without a plan is just a wish." –Antoine de Saint-Exupery

"Give me six hours to chop down a tree and I will spend the first hour sharpening the axe."
–Abraham Lincoln

"A clear vision, backed by definite plans, gives you a tremendous feeling of confidence and personal power." – Brian Tracy

"Keep a little fire burning; however small, however hidden." – Cormac McCarthy

"It is better to take many small steps in the right direction than to make a great leap forward only to stumble backward." –Louis Sacher

"Patience, persistence, and perspiration make an unbeatable combination for success."
 –Napoleon Hill

"Genius is eternal patience." –Michelangelo

"A man who is a master of patience is a master of everything else." –George Savile

Positive Affirmations:

Affirmations have been proven to be effective methods of self-improvement. Basically, Positive affirmations have the ability to change our thought patterns and form new Positive thoughts. Just like physical exercise can form new muscle, Positive affirmations are like an exercise for the brain. We feel good and create a cycle of new Positive thought.

There are many affirmations out there that you can research and look up. Take some time to find some that you love and really speak to you. Here are some examples of ones that I use:

"I am in control of my life and I am creating a new and exciting successful way of living."

"I am full of energy and joy today and I am excited for the opportunities that will come my way."

"I am above negative thoughts and I will not stoop to that level."

"I am full of talent and ambition which I will utilize today."

"I forgive those who have hurt me and I let the pain go, detaching from them peacefully."

"I currently possess all necessary qualities needed to be successful."

"I am good, I am full of life, I am positive, I am perfect in all that I am, and I am ready for success."

"I am so full of positivity that it radiates from me. I attract positivity and positivity is attracted to me."

" Today is going to be amazing."

"I am at peace in my life. At peace with all that has happened, all that is, and all that will be."

Recommended Reading:

These are the most influential books that changed my life and way of thinking and I believe that they can enlighten you as well. In no particular order, here they are:

"How to Win Friends and Influence People" by Dale Carnegie

"The Secret" by Rhonda Byrne

"The Seven Habits of Highly Effective People" by Stephen R. Covey

"Rich Dad, Poor Dad" by Robert Kiyosaki and Sharon Lechter

"Who Moved My Cheese" by Spencer Johnson

"Your Erroneous Zones" by Dr. Wayne W. Dyer

"Think and Grow Rich" by Napoleon Hill

"Chicken Soup for the Soul" by Jack Canfield and Mark Victor Hansen

"The Magic of Thinking Big" by David J. Schwartz

"The Power of Now" by Eckhart Tolle

"See you at the Top" by Zig Ziglar

"The Passion Test" by Chris Attwood and Janet Bray Attwood

"Fearless Passion" by Yong Kang Chan

"Miracles Now" by Gabrielle Bernstein

Recommended Movies or Documentaries
(These were all available on Netflix as of 4-4-17)

"The Secret" 2006

"Fat, Sick, and Nearly Dead" Part 1 and 2, 2010, 2014

"The Kindness Diaries" 2015

Find Me On Social Media

On Instagram: @officialjoshkangley and @hellomynameisjosh_

On Facebook: @officialjoshkangley

On LinkedIn: Joshua S. Kangley

*You can also watch my health journey on YouTube at my channel: drive-thru vegetarian.

19278574R00038

Printed in Poland
by Amazon Fulfillment
Poland Sp. z o.o., Wrocław